W9-CRF-764

SKATEBOARDS
From Start to Finish

Written and Photographed
by Devon Howard

BLACKBIRCH PRESS
An imprint of Thomson Gale, a part of The Thomson Corporation

THOMSON

GALE ™

Detroit • New York • San Francisco • San Diego • New Haven, Conn. • Waterville, Maine • London • Munich

THOMSON

GALE

For Carolina, Harry, and Karen

© 2006 Thomson Gale, a part of The Thomson Corporation.

Thomson and Star Logo are trademarks and Gale and Blackbirch Press are registered trademarks used herein under license.

For more information, contact
Blackbirch Press
27500 Drake Rd.
Farmington Hills, MI 48331-3535
Or you can visit our Internet site at www.gale.com

Photo Credits: Cover, all photos © Devon Howard, except page 3 Time Life Pictures/Getty Images; page 4 (inset), 21 (inset), 31 (inset) Courtesy Sector 9; page 21 © A. McGarry; page 26 © LeRoy Grannis; page 26 (bottom) © Warren Bolster; page 27 © Photo Salas

The author would like to thank Dennis Telfer and the entire Sector 9 crew for their generous support during this project.

LIBRARY OF CONGRESS CATALOGING-IN-PUBLICATION DATA

Howard, Devon.
  Skateboards : from start to finish / by Devon Howard.
    p. cm.
  "SUMMARY: Discusses the step-by-step production process of skateboard building."
  Includes bibliographical references and index.
  ISBN 1-4103-0658-5 (hard cover : alk. paper)
  1. Skateboards—Design and construction—Juvenile literature. I. Title.

TT174.5.S35H69 2005
685'.362—dc22   2005007450

Printed in United States
10 9 8 7 6 5 4 3

Contents

Skateboards

In the 1950s, skateboards were mostly homemade toys. They were usually made with a flat piece of wood fastened with screws to four steel roller-skate wheels. Today's skateboards are made from pressed layers of maple wood, rubber wheels, and special hardware that allows the wheels to turn sharply. Although some skateboards are still homemade, most are built in factories that use the latest tools and building techniques.

Today's skateboards are stronger and easier to ride than ever before. They are also more popular than ever before. More than 12 million people ride skateboards in America alone.

How are skateboards made?

A boy uses roller-skate wheels and a flat piece of wood to make a crude skateboard.

Skateboard Business

Skateboarding is big business. Worldwide, the skateboard industry does nearly $2 billion of business each year. About a dozen companies in the United States build and sell more than 3 million skateboards every year. Sector 9 in San Diego, California, is one of these companies. It has 27 different skateboard models, each one varied in design, length, and width.

Sector 9 makes 27 different skateboard models that vary in design, length, and width.

The Board Source

There are many choices of wood for making skateboards, but maple is considered best because it is light and durable. Most skateboards at Sector 9 are made of Canadian maple wood.

Before the wood even gets to Sector 9, the lumber mill cuts it into thin sheets, or veneers. Using a lathe, which has a fast-spinning blade, the mill slices the maple wood into layers of about $\frac{1}{20}$- to $\frac{1}{16}$-inch (1.27mm to 1.58mm) thick. That is thinner than a tooth pick!

The veneers are shipped from Canada to the Sector 9 factory. There, they will be pressed by a machine and molded into skateboard decks, which are the wooden boards that skateboarders stand on.

Huge stacks of freshly cut Canadian maple wood veneers wait to be pressed into skateboard decks.

5

The Modern Skateboard

All skateboards made today use the same main parts. The deck is the wooden platform that skateboarders stand on. The outer edge, or side, of the deck is called the rail. The front end of a board is called the nose, and the back

The Modern Skateboard

deck

wheel

bearings

trucks

end is known as the tail. Grip tape is applied to the deck's top surface to keep the rider from slipping off.

Trucks are the two metal supports attached to the deck that hold the wheels in place. Trucks have a special design that allows the skateboard to be turned by the rider when he or she leans from one side to the other while standing on the deck.

Every skateboard has four urethane wheels. Inside each wheel, two metal bearings are inserted to make the wheel spin. Bearings are a metal device the size of a quarter and the width of a pencil. They have very tiny metal balls inside them with a lubricant (grease) to help them spin fast on the trucks.

Metal bearings inside these urethane wheels help them spin very fast.

To make the deck, veneers are first placed into a glue spreader machine that applies a special adhesive to both sides of the wood.

Bonding the Wood

Most skateboard decks consist of seven veneers. So, once the veneers arrive at Sector 9, they are organized into stacks of seven. The veneers then need to be glued together. This is done with a glue spreader machine. It applies glue to each side of the veneers except the outside ones, which only get glue on one side. When the veneers exit the spreader, they are ready for the next stage.

Stacks of sticky veneers are ready to be placed in the powerful deck press that will squeeze the veneers together.

Deck Press

The stacks of glued veneers are taken to a deck press machine, which squeezes the veneers together. This machine uses hydraulic pressure to create a tight bond between the seven veneers.

The deck press also bends the veneers to form a slight bow, so that the two ends, or nose and tail, are slightly raised. Wood cannot be melted down like plastic or metal and then poured into a mold. That is why skateboard builders use this technique of gluing veneers together and holding them in their desired shape with a deck press.

After about an hour, the deck can be removed from the press. It will then dry for several days before moving on to the next step.

The deck press uses hydraulic pressure to squeeze the veneers tightly together and bend them into shape.

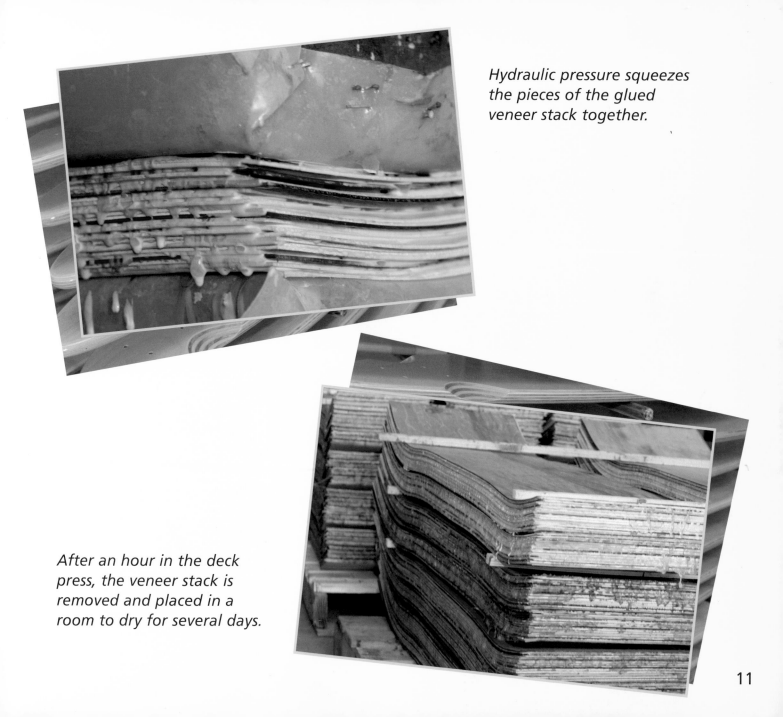

Hydraulic pressure squeezes the pieces of the glued veneer stack together.

After an hour in the deck press, the veneer stack is removed and placed in a room to dry for several days.

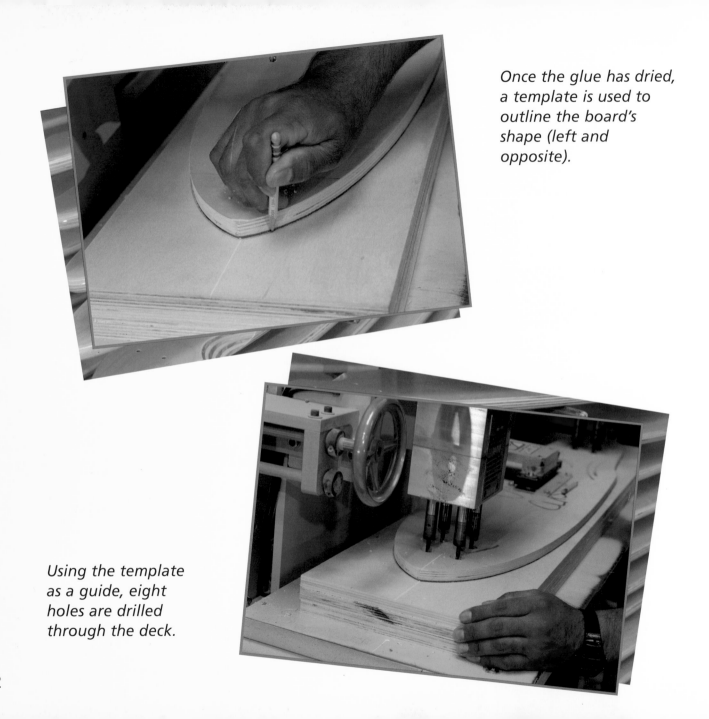

Once the glue has dried, a template is used to outline the board's shape (left and opposite).

Using the template as a guide, eight holes are drilled through the deck.

Drill and Draw

Once the glue has dried, workers prepare for cutting out the board's shape. First, they center a pattern, or template, on the board. Then, using a pen, they trace the outline of the template onto the board.

Once the outline has been marked, the template is removed. Then a drill press is used to make eight holes through the entire veneer stack. Skateboard hardware will be attached to the board's eight holes later in the building process.

A large band saw is used to cut out the rough shape of the board.

The Rough Cut

At this point, it is time to cut out the general shape of the board. The first cut, called a rough cut, traces the outline drawn in pen. This cut is made with a band saw, which uses a long, coarse blade to strip away wood that is outside the template.

Workers guide the veneer stack by hand through the band saw. This part of the building process is very dangerous because there is no safety guard around the blade. To avoid any serious injuries, workers must take extra precautions to keep their fingers, hands, or arms away from the blade.

The very sharp blade cuts the wood right next to the pen line, but this cut is not precise. More cutting and shaving are needed to give the board its final smooth shape.

The band saw's blade stays just outside of the pencil outline while cutting.

Getting Closer

The rough-cut deck is placed on a shaping machine. This machine has a specially designed blade that shaves the rough-cut shape exactly to the template's pen line.

Extra wood on the rough-cut deck (main) must then be removed by the shaping machine (inset).

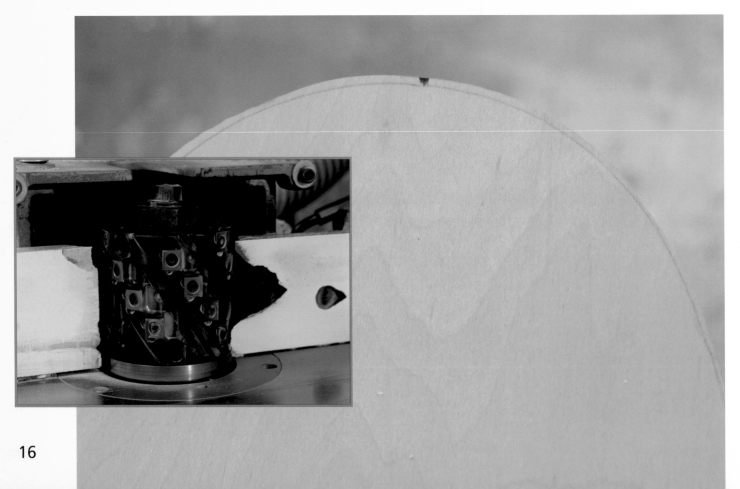

Workers hold the deck with two hands and place the edge of it up to the blade. They control how much the shaping machine cuts into the wood by how much pressure is exerted on the deck. Once the rough areas have been removed, the deck's outline is ready to be finished.

The rough-cut deck is pushed by hand into the shaping machine's rotating blade.

Fine-Tuning

The deck is nearly complete, but a sharp edge around the entire rim, or rail, remains from the shaping machine. Using a router, which has a tiny, spinning blade, workers cut the sharp edge off of the rail.

An air router removes any sharp edges left by the shaping machine (left and below).

With the edge now removed, the entire deck needs to be sanded smooth. Sector 9 uses a drum sander for this job. Fine sand paper is attached to the fast-spinning drum. Workers hold the board's rail, top, and bottom up against the sander. When the sanding is completed, the board has a very smooth finish.

Sector 9 builds an average of 40 skateboards every hour, which amounts to nearly 100,000 skateboards per year!

A drum-sanding machine then smoothes out the entire deck.

History of Sector 9

Sector 9 began in La Jolla, California, in the early 1990s when a group of five surfers started building skateboard decks in their homes. In just a few years, their hobby grew into a million-dollar business. Sector 9 now manufacturers nearly 2,000 skateboards per week. It is now among the leading skateboard brands in the world.

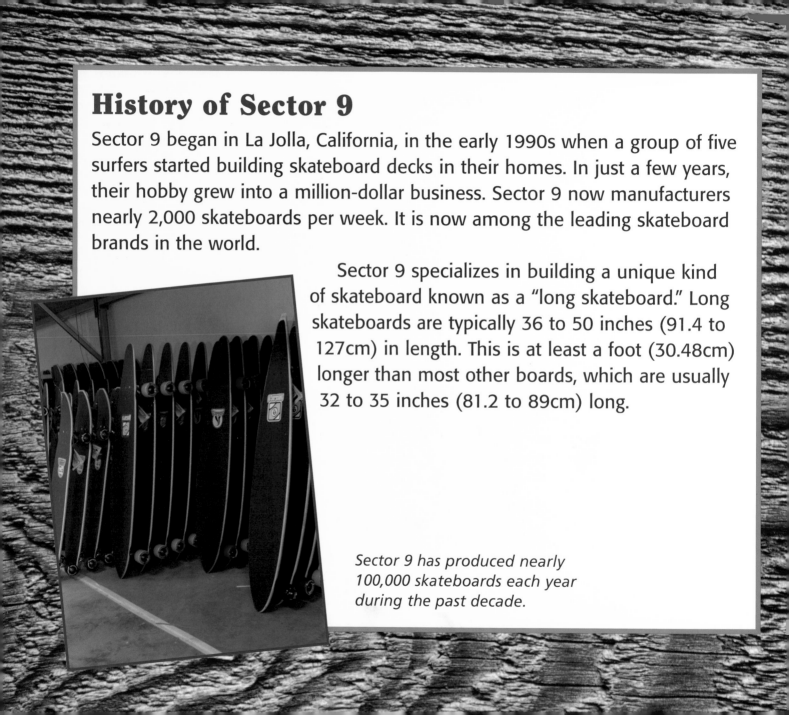

Sector 9 specializes in building a unique kind of skateboard known as a "long skateboard." Long skateboards are typically 36 to 50 inches (91.4 to 127cm) in length. This is at least a foot (30.48cm) longer than most other boards, which are usually 32 to 35 inches (81.2 to 89cm) long.

Sector 9 has produced nearly 100,000 skateboards each year during the past decade.

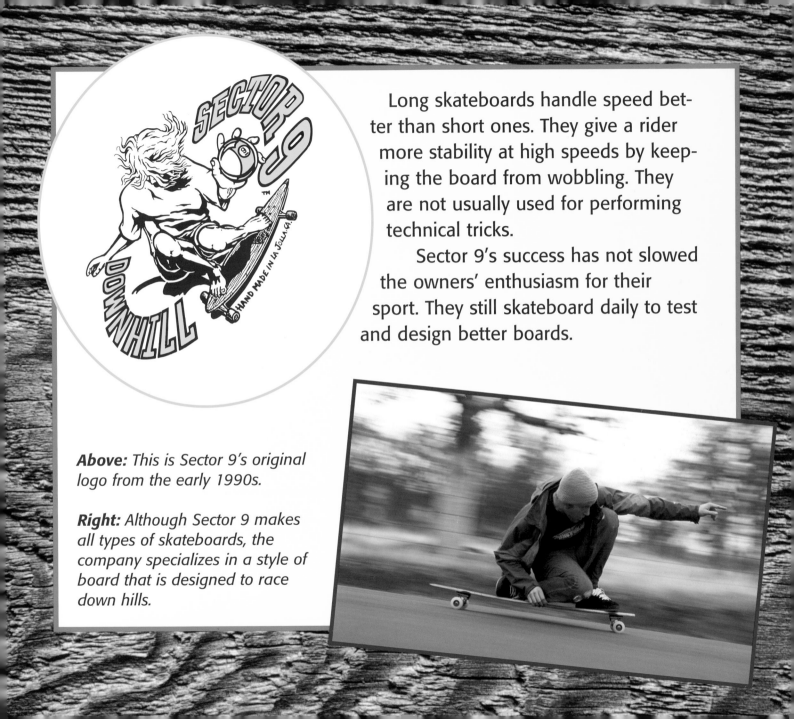

Long skateboards handle speed better than short ones. They give a rider more stability at high speeds by keeping the board from wobbling. They are not usually used for performing technical tricks.

Sector 9's success has not slowed the owners' enthusiasm for their sport. They still skateboard daily to test and design better boards.

Above: This is Sector 9's original logo from the early 1990s.

Right: Although Sector 9 makes all types of skateboards, the company specializes in a style of board that is designed to race down hills.

Sealing the Wood

Once the deck has been sanded, it is then painted with a clear coat of lacquer. The lacquer protects the wood from sun and water damage.

The lacquer is applied with an airbrush inside a room called a spray booth. Workers must wear protective masks while spraying to keep from inhaling the lacquer's harmful vapors. After being sprayed with lacquer, each deck is dried in a rack overnight before the artwork, or graphics, is applied.

The smooth deck is sprayed with a clear coat of lacquer (below). Dozens of boards are then placed on a rack to dry before artwork is applied (opposite).

By the mid 1960s, an estimated 50 million skateboards had been made and sold in America.

Finishing Touches

Most skateboard artwork is created with computer graphics. Sector 9 uses different art for each skateboard model. For example, the Pintail model uses long, colorful stripes for its graphics, while the Cosmic 1 model uses a photograph of a perfect wave. Graphics are usually only placed on the deck's bottom surface. The deck's top surface sometimes has only a small brand logo.

Skateboard artwork is designed using computers.

Graphics are added to the deck with a heat-transfer machine (above). Heat-transfer material hanging over the edge of the deck is carefully removed (right).

There are several methods for adding artwork. Sector 9 generally uses a method known as heat transfer. For heat transfers, the final design is printed by computer onto very thin sheets of specially made plastic. A heat transfer machine then uses heat and compression to attach the sheets to the deck. Any excess plastic hanging off the side of the board is trimmed off with a razor blade.

History of Skateboarding

The earliest examples of skateboardlike vehicles date back to the early 1900s. Back then, kids made scooters by bolting metal roller-skate wheels onto wooden planks and attaching handlebars. What most people know as a skateboard today was not built until the early 1950s. The first boards were designed to simulate surfing on neighborhood sidewalks. By the early 1960s, skateboarding was a nationwide fad, and roughly nine companies were mass-producing skateboards.

After a brief decline in popularity during the late 1960s, skateboarding made a big comeback. In 1974, a revolutionary

Above: The first skateboards were designed to simulate the act of surfing.

Left: In the mid 1970s, a new wheel material called urethane allowed skateboarders to do more radical moves.

new material called urethane was introduced to the sport. Urethane, a soft and durable rubber, became the perfect substance for making skateboard wheels. Almost instantly, urethane wheels made skateboards easier to control. Unlike steel wheels, which caught on every pebble or crack, urethane wheels allowed riders to roll over small obstacles without any trouble. Thanks to this new material, the popularity of skateboarding exploded.

As skateboarding progressed through the 1980s, kids began to master difficult maneuvers with strange names like ollies, hand plants, shuvits, and kick flips. Champion skateboarder Tony Hawk has also helped make skateboarding even more popular around the world. Hawk's Pro Skater game series is one of the best-selling video game series of all time.

There are now over 20 million skateboarders in the world. Skateboarding has risen to the level of surfing and snowboarding as one of the most popular action sports.

Right: *A Sector 9 team rider executes a kick flip.*

Assembly Line

In the last stage of skateboard manufacturing, grip tape and hardware are added. Grip tape is placed on the topside of the deck to provide traction. The hardware is then attached to the finished skateboard deck. Trucks, the supports that hold the wheels in place, are attached to the deck using eight nuts and bolts. Then two metal ball bearings are placed into each wheel. Finally, the four wheels are tightly secured onto the truck axles.

In the last stage of the manufacturing process, grip tape is applied (below), and then the trucks, bearings, and wheels are bolted onto the deck (opposite).

Most skateboarders today are between the ages of 8 and 18.

Completed skateboards are carefully inspected to make sure they are safe to ride.

Ready to Ride

Now that the skateboard is complete, it is almost ready to ride. First, though, it goes through a final inspection to make sure there are no flaws or scratches in the deck. Workers then check to see if there are any missing parts or any loose nuts and bolts. The wheels are also tested to make sure they spin properly.

The completed skateboard is then packed into a box and shipped off to one of the thousands of skateboard shops around the world. It will not be long before some lucky person gets to experience the thrill of the sport on his or her new skateboard!

The boards are finally placed into boxes and shipped to stores all over the world.

Glossary

Drum sander An electric sanding machine that has a rotating cylinder with coarse sandpaper attached

Lathe A cutting machine that firmly holds a piece of wood and turns it while it is being cut

Template The pattern that is used as a guide

Urethane A key ingredient used to make modern skateboard wheels

Veneer An extremely thin layer of wood, usually made by a lathe

For More Information

Books
Jamie Brisick, *Have Board, Will Travel: The Definitive History of Surf, Skate, and Snow*. New York: HarperCollins Quicksilver, 2004.

Michael Brooke, *Concrete Wave: The History of Skateboarding*. Vancouver, Canada: Warwick, 1999.

Rhyn Noll, *Skateboard Retrospective: A Collector's Guide*. Atglen, PA: Schiffer, 2000.

——, *Skateboarding: Past, Present, Future*. Atglen, PA: Schiffer, 2003.

Web Sites
(www.sector9.com). Learn more about Sector 9 and see all of its different skateboard models and accessories through this Web site.

(www.skateboard.about.com). This is a great place to start learning the basics about skateboarding. Learn what all the different parts of the skateboard are and how they work. Also learn about skateboard history, culture, and the types of tricks that skateboarders do.

Index